The Gentle Rain from Heaven

by
Mark Nicholls

This first edition published in Australia in 2019 by:

Prahran Publishing
P.O. Box 2041, Prahran, Victoria, 3181

© Copyright Mark Nicholls 2019

Mark Nicholls has asserted his legal and moral right under the Copyright Act 1968 to be identified as the author of this work.

Published by arrangement with
Prahran Publishing, Australia.

All rights are strictly reserved.

No part of this publication may be reproduced, stored in a retrieval system or transmitted, in any form or by any other means, without the publisher's prior permission in writing. Copying of this script for performance reasons is also strictly prohibited by law, either in whole or excerpts from.

This book is sold subject to the condition that it shall not, by way of trade or otherwise, be lent, resold, hired out or otherwise circulated without the publisher's prior consent in any form of binding or cover other than that in which it is published and without similar condition, including this condition, being imposed on the subsequent purchaser.

Every reasonable effort has been made to trace copyright holders of material reproduced in this book, but if any have been inadvertently overlooked the publishers would be glad to hear from them. The story, all names, characters, and incidents portrayed in this book are fictitious. No identification with actual persons past or present, places, buildings, and products is intended or should be inferred.

ISBN 978-1-922263-18-6 Paperback
ISBN 978-1-922263-19-3 eBook

Dewey: 822.4

A catalogue record for this book is available from the National Library of Australia

Performance Licensing and Royalty Payments

Mark Nicholls retains control of both the amateur and professional stage performance rights of this play. No unauthorised performance should occur without the express and written permission of the playwright.

Restriction of Alteration

There shall be no modifications of any kind to the play including deletion of dialogue (including objectionable language), changes to characters gender or names, title of the play or music without the express and written permission from the author.

Sound and Video Recordings

This play may contain stage directions to include the use of music, video or other sound recordings either in part or in whole. The author and the publisher have not sought the right to use such content and performance rights permission should be obtained separately. Permission to record audio and video recordings of all performances must also be explicitly given by the author in writing.

Author Credit

Performance rights approval requires credit be given to Mark Nicholls as the sole and exclusive author of the play. This obligation applies to the title page of every program or other advertising material distributed in connection to this play. The author's credit should appear immediately under the title of the play on all published material, and alongside no other individual. Font size of credit cannot be less than 50% of the largest letter used in the play's title.

Please email info@prahran.press
for all performance enquiries.

Dedication

for Ali Wirtz

About the Playwright

MARK NICHOLLS has been performing on various Melbourne stages since the age of six and has an extensive list of credits as a playwright, composer, singer, actor, producer and director. He is Senior Lecturer in Cinema Studies at the University of Melbourne where he has taught film since 1993.

He is the author of *Lost Objects of Desire: The Performances of Jeremy Irons* (2012), *Scorsese's Men: Melancholia and the Mob* (2004) and recently published articles on Italian Cinema, Powell and Pressburger's *The Red Shoes* and Sergei Diaghilev's celebrated company, The Ballets Russes.

Mark is a film critic and worked for many years on ABC Radio and for *The Age* newspaper, for which he wrote a weekly column between 2007 and 2009.

He lives in Melbourne with his partner, Ali Wirtz, and their two sons Oscar and Carlo.

Series Preface

I wrote these plays for only one reason, to perform them. I publish them here, therefore, somewhat reluctantly. They were never written to be read on the page by anyone but a treasured posy of performers that I trust to help me rescue them from it. They were certainly never conceived of as works of anything so respectable as literature. Nevertheless, I have found two reasons to overcome my reluctance and my usual roguish prejudice against readers and writers in favour of performers and punters. One reason is that putting these plays into print provides the opportunity for the most engaged of those who saw and heard them to revive and revise the experience. The other reason is archival. I wish to leave a permanent, if inadequate, record of the facts of their production over a decade, in a private space in Melbourne, for the benefit of both a small, dedicated paying audience, and for a smaller band of compulsive show-folk.

Writing these plays for the talented actors, musicians and backstage characters whose creations are recorded here, and having the privilege of working with these artists to produce them, has been the most satisfying occupation of my otherwise horrendously charmed and fascinating life.

Now that they have had their blessed release in print, these plays are beyond the concern of any motivation I had to write them. Read them, o curious one, and work it out for yourself! One motivation I will record, however, rests in the inspiration generously given by those who worked on and attended these cosy performances, and so brought their privileged, fleeting moments of theatre securely into being.

About the Play

In the early 2000s I read a news story about a situation not unlike that presented in this play. As a bit of self-protective censorship, I might have easily passed over it. The reason I did not was that I noticed that the government official sent to deal with this case was at the very same diplomatic level as a good friend of mine, let's call him Alex, recently sent on his very first posting. That the story stayed with me is obviously due to an element of empathy. I am not quite sure that it is entirely a matter of empathy for the victims of this horrendous crime. In fact, if I am completely honest with myself, it was probably more a matter of thinking 'Better Alex than me.'

Writing this introduction in Melbourne in March 2019, it strikes me that we are often not very good at listening to the stories of victims of all too believable cruelty. When the powerful, the great and the good take up arms against such victims, for whatever agendas they may be pursuing, we are all entitled to join with such victims in feeling a degree of paranoia that would not be out of place in a Kafka story.

As a victim of trauma in this play, no doubt John has horrible nightmares and experiences a degree of such paranoia. Many victims have the irresistible option of staying quiet and doing nothing. As a victim seeking at least some form of recognition, John has a rare luxury. Doing nothing will not simply condemn him to a lifetime of quiet pain and alienation. Doing nothing, in John's case, will bring about the most violent and extreme form of public justice imaginable. Given what he and his daughter suffered, the idea that anyone, especially the Australian Government, would presume to question any particular legal course of action he may pursue may be thought to be profoundly demoralising. Margaret certainly comes to this conclusion. It is just lucky that through John's superior sense of altruism we get the result that, I assume, we all hope for.

We went back and forth over this in rehearsal. As director, writer and the actor playing John, I don't think I really settled on this result until a few days before we opened. The temptation to leave John's final decision ambiguous was overwhelming. I certainly wrote it that way in the first place. I am pretty sure it was Madeleine Swain, playing Margaret, whose experience and sound theatrical sense made the decision that John should put us all out of our misery. I remain certain that this was the right theatrical decision. I am even more certain that it is true to life. I just wish I could be certain that these sorts decisions, so obvious to most of us, are always the right ones.

Characters

John:	forty-eight
Athena:	twenty, then twenty-five, then twenty-six
Margaret:	fifty-two
Nina:	twenty-three

Setting

Now in a hospital morgue, a hotel room and in the Australian Embassy in Riyadh, Saudi Arabia. Also six years past and one year past in a house in Melbourne.

The Gentle Rain From Heaven was first performed at Rear 4, Clifton Hill, Victoria on 22nd February, 2017 with the following cast:

John:	Mark Nicholls
Athena:	Evangeline Stoios
Margaret:	Madeleine Swain
Nina:	Helena Duniec

Director:	Mark Nicholls
Stage Manager:	Oscar Wirtz
Assistant Stage Manager:	Carlo Nicholls
Co Producer:	Alison Wirtz

Prologue

The lights come up on a morgue scene in which a dead body of a woman, covered by a thin sheet, is lying on a table. In time, JOHN enters. Eventually he pulls back the sheet covering her face, as if peeling away a thin sheet of dead skin. He looks at her with facination, which turns, in time, to utter despair. He cannot cry but begins to gasp for air, breathing deeply over and over again. Finally, he composes himself to the extent to which he can move. He leaves but stops himself just before exiting. Without looking back at her, as he no doubt did thousands of times during her childhood:

JOHN: Goodnight, my love.

Exits.

End Prologue.

Act One

The lounge area of a large hotel suite, with the bedroom and bathroom stage left. NINA and MARGARET enter lugging their own bags.

NINA: Why the mad rush to get up here? I'm sure we could have got someone to bring up the bags if we had waited a minute.

MARGARET: Yes, I know. But I'm not really sure about the tipping, so I thought it was best to avoid the whole business.

NINA: Surely they covered local etiquette in your pre-posting training?

MARGARET: Yes, but it was all about how to eat bananas standing up, and what to do with the cherry stones when you are sitting down. They didn't cover anything so useful as how much to tip or what voltage to anticipate for your hair-straightener.

NINA: I think that's all pretty much covered on the website, Mum.

MARGARET: Darling, I'm a junior Australian Government official seconded to a foreign Embassy. They don't let me have access to anything nearly so sensitive as Aussietraveller.gov.au.

NINA: That bodes well for your assignment.

MARGARET: No, but that's just it. They only tell us exactly what we need to know. I'm sure it's a hangover from the old espionage days. If we had all that really useful information we might find ourselves in terrible danger.

NINA: What, you might be taken for someone who really knows what they are doing?

MARGARET: Precisely.

NINA: I'm seeing *The Guardian* headlines now. 'Third secretary exposes Lady Shaver voltage: blows deep cover for thousands of double agents behind enemy lines.'

MARGARET: Something like that, yes.

NINA: Is there really any of that interesting business left? I thought it was all just boring trade stuff and passports.

MARGARET: Pretty much. But it does make a nice change from hosing down the collective testosterone rush of year nine boys in seventh period on Friday.

NINA: *[Looking about the suite]* And you'd have to say this is all looking pretty good. Not a bad pad for your first posting.

MARGARET: It's only for a few days and then we are back in Canberra. If I ever do get a real overseas posting, and I can actually convince your father to come with me, I doubt that they will be turning on anything like this in the way of accommodation. A boxy little Soviet-

	era flat and an incompetent housekeeper cum secret service informant, checking over your rubbish bins, is usually the norm I think.

NINA: Still this is pretty good. The department are obviously keen for you to be comfortable so you do a good job here.

MARGARET: No, I think someone just took pity on me because the whole thing is such a non-event. They probably tried to nobble someone else with a three-star hotel offer and struck out. I suspect they bumped the accommodation up to five-star to make sure the schmuck was in the bag.

NINA: And you're the schmuck?

MARGARET: Embarrassing but true.

NINA: And they don't really care what happens with this bloke and his dead daughter?

MARGARET: I don't think so.

NINA: That's appalling.

MARGARET: I don't mean it like that. But from what I was told, it is all really about the paperwork and making sure someone is flying the Canberra flag if the media get into it.

NINA: Well, what happens if it does end up in an execution?

MARGARET: Apparently that's unlikely.

NINA:	But it's a possibility. Perhaps that's why they sent you. If it does end in a 'judicial murder' no one in the embassy here ends up with egg on their face.
MARGARET:	*[A trifle concerned]* They said not.
NINA:	Well, they would, wouldn't they?
MARGARET:	I'm sure it's not like that.
NINA:	What, so you're here simply to meet up with this bloke, remind him that he has the option to have his daughter's rapist and murderer executed by beheading or to let him walk free. Then get your bloke to sign up for clemency, presumably without any problems at all?
MARGARET:	That's the general idea.
NINA:	Did anyone think that it could go the other way?
MARGARET:	No. I think they are pretty sure of my 'bloke'.
NINA:	What's his name again?
MARGARET:	*[Digging in her case]* Oh, hang on, let me look it up, I've forgotten.
NINA:	Yeah well actually it's John Ferguson. He's 48, I think he's a lawyer or something, one daughter – *had* one daughter – and his wife Louise died of breast cancer six years ago.
MARGARET:	Yes, I knew all that.

NINA:	Did you?
MARGARET:	Yes, of course. I just forgot the name.
NINA:	Well, does anyone at DFAT know it. I mean above the level of canteen staff.
MARGARET:	Of course they do.
NINA:	So, they know he's not going to go the other way?
MARGARET:	I'm sure. Otherwise they would hardly be sending me in.
NINA:	Why, because they think he's a 'good bloke', do they?
MARGARET:	We checked him out. This bloke is literally a scout master.
NINA:	Yeah, I wonder what Baden-Powell thought of judicial murder and the death penalty!
MARGARET:	I don't mean that. I mean, this bloke literally spends his weekends coaching Auskick and doing the Sunday shift for Meals on Wheels.
NINA:	What, Auskick's now a chapter of Amnesty International, is it? They make them memorise the UN Charter on Human Rights and recite it as part of the pre-match entertainment?

MARGARET: Well, of course, it's true, they are not all spending their Sunday mornings at single-origin pop-ups on Smith Street. But I think we can assume that they are not all card-carrying feral rednecks.

NINA: That's not what I mean.

MARGARET: Well, what do you mean?

NINA: Hasn't anyone considered that this bloke may not want his daughter's murderer to walk away from this? And without being either here or there on the finer points of international human rights law, he might just as well say 'stuff it, let the bastard die'.

MARGARET: Apparently that is not the way it is going to go.

NINA: I certainly hope so.

MARGARET: What, for the murderer's sake?

NINA: Yes, actually. But I'm probably more concerned for Ferguson.

MARGARET: Why exactly? He is not facing the executioner.

NINA: Well, let's say he does let them cut the bastard's head off. How do you think he's going to feel when he wakes up out of his haze of vengeance in about three years, feels no better for having conspired in a judicial murder and still finds himself without his daughter – let alone his wife.

MARGARET: Either way, I don't know how he is going to feel.

NINA: How are you going to feel, Mum?

MARGARET: About what?

NINA: About John Ferguson, no daughter, no wife and a judicial murder on his conscience, just to mix up the emotional cocktail a bit.

MARGARET: I wish you'd stop calling it 'judicial murder'.

NINA: Well, that's what it is, isn't it?

MARGARET: It might be what they call it in the caf at Uni, but I can assure you no one calls it that in DFAT. *[Pause]* Anyway, who knows? Maybe it will be of some comfort.

NINA: Yes, it is always of some potential comfort to other people. But people never really think that for themselves.

MARGARET: Well, in that case, I will have to rely on the fact that I am spectacularly unqualified and seek the right type of counsel.

NINA: And where will you get that?

MARGARET: Why do you think I brought you with me?

NINA: I'm not going to be much help. My law degree – such as it is – is not going to get you out of this. Anyway, I am really only here for the mini-bar.

MARGARET: Well, that is good, because it's free.

NINA: Really?

MARGARET: Yeah. I think they are willing to spot us for the price of an orange juice or two.

NINA: *[Remembering Islamic law]* Ah, that's right. Damn.

MARGARET: Back to Aussietraveller.gov.au for you, my love.

End Act.

Act Two

Six years earlier. JOHN is sitting, as if in shock, at a large dining table, with a 'spread' before him, as found at a wake or post funeral event. ATHENA is offstage getting rid of the last of the guests.

GUEST 1: *[NINA off]* Now you look after that poor father of yours, Athena. He's clearly in shock and we don't want him getting sick.

ATHENA: *[Off]* Goodbye, Mrs Shore. Yes, I'll do my best. I think it will take some time, but I'm sure we can look after each other.

GUEST 2: *[MARGARET off]* Yes, poor John. You must look after him. It will take him weeks to get over this. You know when my Wolf died I was incapable of anything for at least a month. In fact, I'm still not feeling a 100 percent. Dead at 91. Can you believe it?

ATHENA: *[Off]* Oh, I'm so sorry Mrs Black. I hope you'll rally soon.

GUEST 2: *[MARGARET off]* Thank you, dear. But life goes on.

There is a pause as we hear the door being closed and ATHENA enters. She sits opposite her father, but neither says a word for a while. Then they burst out laughing.

JOHN: That is the last wake I am either hosting or attending.

ATHENA: It's really quite disgusting how much grieving goes on at a funeral. And none of it has anything to do with the woman in the box.

JOHN: That's got to be the best spot in the house though. Centre stage, isolated, no one can get at you and you can just lie there and let the whole thing wash over you.

ATHENA: Literally. *[Pause]* Do you actually think she was in there?

JOHN: The funeral director said so. I made sure with him.

ATHENA: Yeah, I don't know. I can't imagine Mum there at all.

JOHN: What you think she did some escape routine?

ATHENA: Well you would, wouldn't you?

JOHN: Can you imagine how awful it would be to have your friends 'pouring out' tributes to you.

ATHENA: Well, at least we spared her that.

JOHN: Well you certainly did with your eulogy. Is your mother's funeral really the time to start speculating in public about whether or not she was hot for your boyfriend?

ATHENA:	That worked like a charm. Saved a lot of awkward chatter. By the time we got back here that's all anyone really wanted to talk about.
JOHN:	Not in my part of the room. All I got was people complaining about their health and how sad they were when their dog died.
ATHENA:	Yes, funerals are really just an obligation to facilitate and subsidise everyone else in their shabby little moments of grief. Can you honestly say you feel any better or worse for having done it?
JOHN:	No. I just feel exhausted.
ATHENA:	Me too. In fact, I think the only thing we really got out of it was a low brick fence load of lasagne.
JOHN:	All riddled with mushroom and tidal waves of tasteless béchamel, no doubt.
ATHENA:	Well, at least it will spare us the onslaught of kindly folk 'popping in' with food for the next three weeks.
JOHN:	No, I think my 'overcome with grief' bit made sure that was never going to happen. We'll be taboo for at least three months.
ATHENA:	I was impressed with your 'so overcome with grief that tears fail' approach to the job.
JOHN:	Really? That's textbook. Your proffering the cougar thesis was the real stroke of genius.

ATHENA: *[She picks up an open champagne bottle and pours two glasses]* We are good at this, aren't we! *[Gives him a glass and takes one herself]* Here's to us.

JOHN: Here's to us. And here's to Mum.

ATHENA: Yes. Here's to you, Mum. A life very thoroughly lived – and a quick exit.

JOHN: Ruthlessly quick.

ATHENA: Was it just me, or did you keep expecting Mum's other family to emerge?

JOHN: *[Laughing]* I forgot about that one. No, I just keep trying to avoid anyone with your complexion who looked like an ex-boyfriend.

ATHENA: Ah yes, my *[Gesturing]* 'real father'.

JOHN: Everyone was so full of their own stuff in that church, I wouldn't have put it past some washed-up poet hippy thinking it was just the right moment to make a clean breast of it.

ATHENA: I didn't see any desirable candidates in the church for that job. I'll just have to stick with you for the moment.

A pause.

JOHN: So, what do we have to do now?

ATHENA: There's nothing we need to do.

JOHN:	So, what do we do?
ATHENA:	Whatever you want to do.
JOHN:	I have absolutely no idea what that is.
ATHENA:	Yes. Mum said you wouldn't.
JOHN:	Did she? When?
ATHENA:	When she got sick. We had a discussion about it, and about the future.
JOHN:	What did she think?
ATHENA:	She thought you might be tempted to let all this define you. To make an occupation out of grief.
JOHN:	Well, it has been known.
ATHENA:	Of course it has. But she wanted you to go the other way.
JOHN:	And how do I do that, exactly?
ATHENA:	She wanted me to tell you to think of all the times over the years that you longed to be alone, to run off with a surfie chick, to get away from her and her illness *[Pause]* to let her go, to let her off the hook of having to love you.
JOHN:	And then what?
ATHENA:	Then do it.

JOHN: It's just pretty hard to remember ever thinking about that.

ATHENA: You're not being honest then. What was your relationship with Mum if you didn't want to chuck each other off a cliff from time to time?

JOHN: It just doesn't seem like much to go on with.

ATHENA: Really? You don't think being abandoned by death can be a little bit like being abandoned by divorce? Are you so sophisticated that you think you are beyond entertaining hostility towards the dead? I can tell you I'm not. I'm not really feeling that much at the moment, but I am mad as hell with her right now.

JOHN: Perhaps.

ATHENA: Well, there's something to work with.

Pause.

JOHN: Did she really say that?

ATHENA: Of course not. What, do you think she was nuts? She probably wants you tearing the flesh and wearing the widower's weeds like any normal person.

JOHN: So where did all that come from?

ATHENA: It came from me. I am telling you to do this – but I am sure if Mum were about and thinking straight she'd agree with me, although she never said it. *[Pause]* Look, I'm not thinking particularly clearly, obviously. Listening to all those old dears today carrying on about my 'poor father', all I really wanted to say was, "Doesn't anyone seem to realise that that is my mother in that bloody box? It's not some stranger, like a husband or wife, that I met at a party one night and got yoked to in order to alleviate the mortgage payments. That woman is the woman who carried me inside her body for nine months then couldn't get me out of her mind for the next twenty years. Not for one moment. Not until the second she died. So just shut up about Dad, and your 90-year-old husband and your bloody cat. There's nothing inside that box which doesn't belong to me – and I am never getting it back." *[Pause]* So I'm not thinking particularly clearly. But I am thinking, and whatever this moment is, it has to be worth something. I suppose I have this terrible, almost guilty feeling that there is actually something quite exciting about all this. That her death is some sick sort of beneficence – 'the gentle rain from heaven'. That, if we can, somehow, make our way through all the grief and the loss and the sheer physical exhaustion of it all, that it's going to be something quite extraordinary for us. That we are going to live the rest of our lives with some sort of knowledge that very few people have – or at least realise they have. We have to make the most of it. We really have to.

JOHN embraces her without a word.

End Act.

Entre' Act

ATHENA (SINGS)

Carefully and silently
I sing my song of loneliness.
You stand still and calmly listen
No one knows you're there.

Tell me all your daily rhythms
Let me know of all your cares.
Fill my mind with deepest longings
Fathom your despair.

Name three things that came between us
I'll catalogue my sins too.
Beg a tender blessing of me
I'll beg one of you.

Shun confusion, pride, delusion
Pity weakness, greed forswear.
Promise nothing more than this, Dear
Promise to be there.

Carefully and silently
I sing my song of loneliness.
You stand still and calmly listen
No one knows you're there.

End Entre'Act.

Act Three

The lights are low as NINA enters the hotel suite so we can hardly see. MARGARET is lying on her bed offstage, in the dark with the curtains shut. Stumbling over something, NINA turns on a light.

MARGARET: Please don't turn them on.

NINA: Oh, good Lord. I didn't see you.

MARGARET: That's all right. Just let me lie here for a while in the dark.

NINA: OK. *[She turns the lights down]* What's the matter? Have you got a headache?

MARGARET: The headache is the good news.

NINA: What is the bad news?

MARGARET: I saw John Ferguson today.

NINA: Do I assume it was not quite the success you anticipated?

MARGARET: It was not.

NINA: What did he say?

MARGARET: Very little.

NINA: Given what he's been though, it's hardly surprising that he's not exactly chatty.

MARGARET: Oh, I'm sure he would have been quite forthcoming on the state of the economy, the Republican debate, or the Essendon Football Club doping scandal, but he has absolutely nothing to say on the subject of his daughter's death.

NINA: Nothing?

MARGARET: Nothing.

NINA: He's not aphasic?

MARGARET: Not that I could tell. No, he just refuses to talk about what I want to talk about.

NINA: So, he had nothing to say on the subject?

MARGARET: Nothing *[Pause]* except that he has no intention of doing anything to stop the execution.

NINA: Well, what else do you want? Surely after making a statement like that he must have pretty much accrued enough conversational credits to last him a while?

MARGARET: I suppose so.

NINA: How long were you with him?

MARGARET: About 10 minutes.

NINA: Ten minutes? That's almost perverse for you. It usually takes you that long to get past the weather, what you had for lunch and all the other polite introductories you're so keen on.

MARGARET: Not with this bloke. On this topic, there are no possible avenues of small talk.

NINA: What so you just kicked off with it? "Hello Mr Ferguson, I'm Margaret from DFAT. Um, re: that judicial murder, ah execution, you are involved in – any chance of not going in that particular direction?"

MARGARET: It wasn't exactly like that.

NINA: There couldn't have been much time for anything else in 10 minutes.

MARGARET: Oh, my head is killing me.

NINA: Did you take something?

MARGARET: Several things.

NINA: I suppose they will kick in in a moment.

MARGARET: I have been anticipating that for an hour.

She gets up and joins NINA in the lounge.

NINA: Are you sure it's a good idea to get up?

MARGARET: I think it's worse lying down.

NINA: So that was all you got out of him?

MARGARET: Yes. I asked him if he was aware of the situation. He said he was. I asked him whether he was thinking about clemency. He said he wasn't.

NINA: What did you do then?

MARGARET: Frankly, I was somewhat bowled over.

NINA: But you knew that was a possibility.

MARGARET: Not by what he said. Just the way he said it. He wasn't frothing at the mouth or screaming for blood. He just came out with it quietly and calmly.

NINA: Forget it. He's obviously still in shock. So, what did you say to the 'quietly and calmly'?

MARGARET: I asked him whether he wanted to talk about it. He said that he had no desire to, and that he just wanted to go. So I opened the door and he walked out.

NINA: You let him go?

MARGARET: He's not under arrest. He's not under any obligation to talk to me at all.

NINA: I suppose not. But for someone formerly expert in cornering Year Nine boys and force-feeding them Wilfred Owen, I would have thought you might have been a little more adept with this bloke.

MARGARET: By then it was far too late. I stuffed up. Clearly I took the wrong line from the beginning and, once I realised it, there was no going back.

NINA: Hence the headache and the darkened room.

MARGARET:	Precisely. *[Pause]* And they do Sassoon now.
NINA:	What?
MARGARET:	Siegfried Sassoon. Year Nine.
NINA:	What happened to Wilfred Owen?
MARGARET:	Owen's out, Sassoon's in.
NINA:	I suppose that is about right, really. But, gee, it must be hard work for a poet on the Western Front. The moment you think you've got the Germans sorted out in front of you, you have to start worrying about the National Curriculum attacking from the rear.
MARGARET:	Now you know why I was invalided out.

[Pause]

NINA:	Well, I have to say that it all feels something of an anticlimax. What happens now? Do we just repack our bags, avoid the porter and head for the airport?
MARGARET:	No. I managed to delay that by pretending that I had to get him to sign some papers. So he has agreed to meet me on Tuesday, for 15 minutes.
NINA:	As long as that? Better make those papers up in triplicate or you might be struggling to make it to 15 minutes.

MARGARET: Quite.

NINA: Still, given your form today, that particular move has got to earn you at least some credit towards the whole business.

MARGARET: Not much.

NINA: Well, what are you going to do in 15 minutes?

MARGARET: I have no idea. I'm too depressed. How do you talk someone down from this in 15 minutes?

NINA: So that's an issue now is it?

MARGARET: What on earth do you mean?

NINA: Well, the other day it seemed that talking him down was really just a bit of unnecessary business.

MARGARET: Well it was, in a way. We had absolutely no idea that it was going to be necessary.

NINA: And now it is?

MARGARET: Why do you think I've got this headache?

NINA: Because it's all madly inconvenient.

MARGARET: That's not it and you know it.

NINA: Do I? I wasn't 100 percent sure of you a few days ago.

MARGARET: I wish you would stop going on about that. A few days ago we had no reason to expect we had a problem.

NINA: *[Interrupting]* Why do you keep saying we? You're not in the Mafia.

MARGARET: I had no reason to think Ferguson was going to be a problem. It was probably wishful thinking, but it seemed to work at the time. I suppose I didn't really want to deal with the horrible alternative until I had to. It's far too awful to think about. Now I have to think about it and if you want to be any help you need to stop this DFAT bashing thing and talk it over with me. You're far too late with that gag anyway – *Yes Minister* did it in the early eighties.

NINA: I just want to make sure we are not looking out for any interests but Ferguson's?

MARGARET: We're not. Although, quite clearly, we are playing a reasonably supportive role on behalf of the rapist.

NINA: What's he like?

MARGARET: I've never met him.

NINA: Not the rapist. Ferguson.

MARGARET: Well, you can forget the Auskick and the Meals on Wheels

NINA: What do you mean?

MARGARET: I'd say he was more into contemporary classical music and Italian neo-Futurist design.

NINA: What, an aesthete?

MARGARET: Something like that.

NINA: That's funny. You made him out to be some sort of minimal variation on your basic Aussie bloke. Clean, tidy, no excess hair and looking slightly out of place in leisure wear.

MARGARET: Well, you can forget that. This fellow is deep and reflective.

NINA: And that is a more difficult prospect than footy dad and nice to old folk?

MARGARET: You really don't give me credit for very much you know. I know I am just an ex-high school teacher, but I have been about a bit. I didn't just come down in the last shower of the National Curriculum. I too was once a beautiful university graduate, had parents, grandparents, sleazy Christmas Day uncles, and sometimes got held up by ladies with pink and purple hair at the church fete. I think I have at least something to contribute in the way of people skills.

NINA: Just wanted to make sure we weren't indulging in folksy fairy tales when simple suburban folk meet up with their destiny and high foreign affairs.

MARGARET: That's ridiculous.

Act III

NINA: Is it? You'd have to say it's been a pretty significant theme in the discourse until now. Anyway, what has he to be so deep and reflective about?

MARGARET: You mean apart from his daughter?

NINA: I didn't mean that.

Pause.

MARGARET: Have you thought about her much?

NINA: To be honest, I don't think I have.

MARGARET: It's easier not to isn't it?

NINA: Effortlessly easier.

MARGARET: Yes. It leaves the clemency issue much less cloudy.

NINA: It does?

MARGARET: Do you think that's fair?

NINA: Who to?

MARGARET: The daughter. Her name was Athena.

NINA: What, is it unfair to concentrate on the death penalty issues rather than to concentrate on her suffering?

MARGARET: No. That's obviously not fair – although I have the most horrific suspicion that it might actually be just. No, I'm thinking it's not exactly fair for us to sideline her suffering simply because we can't bear to think about it.

NINA: Well, I can't bear to think about it. Can you?

MARGARET: No.

NINA: Do you know what actually happened?

MARGARET: Yes. Sort of.

NINA: *[Reluctantly]* What happened?

MARGARET: I can't bear to say.

NINA: Really?

MARGARET: Yes, really. I just can't. I have this terrible feeling that if I speak about it out loud, I'll never get rid of it.

NINA: And you won't be able to do your job?

MARGARET: I don't really care about that. In fact, I don't really know what I think about the death penalty in amongst all of this. I think you were right the other day – another dead body is no good to our 'bloke'. Even if he doesn't know it.

NINA: I am sure that's right.

End Act.

Entr'Act

NINA (SINGS)

The moon shines bright. In such a night
as this,
When the sweet wind did gently kiss the trees
And they did make no noise.

The moon shines bright. In such a night
as this,
Wise Athene walked softly in the night
And was n'er seen again.

The moon shines bright. In such a night
as this,
Did proud John sigh and call his love to heel
And lost his love anew.

The moon shines bright. In such a night
as this,
Was Margaret firm and loath to lose a tear
Yet she lay down to weep.

The moon shines bright. In such a night
as this,
Di Nina laugh and unearth another lie
As wise Ath'en again.

The moon shines bright. In such a night
as this,
When the sweet wind did gently kiss the trees
And they did make no noise.

End Entr'Act.

Act Four

A year earlier. ATHENA and JOHN are playing table tennis.

ATHENA: Nine-two your way. Come on Dad. You can't possible lose this.

JOHN: You have been saying that for an hour.

ATHENA: I say that every time we play.

JOHN: Yes, you always say it, but you never do anything to make it happen.

ATHENA: That's your job.

JOHN: Well, I obviously can't pull it off by myself. You could help me out a bit.

ATHENA: I always intend to, but then I just can't stop myself. I see a weak backhand shot and the exposed left side of the table and I have to smash it. It's something animal in me. My head says 'hit and giggle', but my heart says 'survival of the fittest'. Nature really is savage, isn't it?

JOHN: Undoubtedly. *[They continue playing in silence for a moment until someone wins a point]* What were you doing all day?

ATHENA: Various things.

JOHN: Anything newsworthy.

ATHENA: Are we talking national or domestic consumption?

JOHN: Domestic.

ATHENA: I think you mean domestic, but I mean national.

JOHN: Whichever.

ATHENA: Well, I had a job interview.

JOHN: Where?

ATHENA: Skype.

JOHN: The Alfred not putting out for the price of a tram fare nowadays?

ATHENA: It wasn't with anyone in Prahran.

JOHN: Where was it?

ATHENA: Actually, it was a company based in London.

JOHN: Really? Are you thinking of moving to London?

ATHENA: Not at all. I'm thinking of moving to Riyadh, Saudi Arabia.

JOHN: Why there?

ATHENA: The money is good. And they need nurses.

JOHN: Don't they need nurses at the Alfred?

ATHENA:	Not really. In fact, they really need them in Lower Snug, Tasmania more than anywhere, but that is not what we are talking about is it?
JOHN:	You mean we're talking about money?
ATHENA:	Not at all. At least you aren't.
JOHN:	What am I talking about?
ATHENA:	You're talking about letting me go.
JOHN:	Am I?
ATHENA:	You are. I'm talking about 18 months in Saudi to make some money so I can put a deposit on a house. You're talking about how on Earth you can cope with the idea of letting me go.
JOHN:	It's not up to me to 'let you go' or 'make you stay', for that matter.
ATHENA:	Of course it's not. It's about you simply opening up your mind to the possibility of me not sleeping in the next room, or at least the next suburb.
JOHN:	Is that so odd, for a parent?
ATHENA:	It's not odd at all. In most cases it's kind of natural.
JOHN:	But in my case?

ATHENA: In your case it's tinged by your experience of loss. I know you try really hard to cover it over, but I see you. That little extra back straightening and manly fist-clenching you used to do when I left for school every day. The 'have a good time' when I went out with my friends at night, which really meant 'don't have too good a time' – and the relief when I got home and you were pretending to be asleep. I know you. You are a secret control freak.

JOHN: I'm sorry. That all must be really hard for you. I always really tried to not let you see any of that.

ATHENA: I know.

JOHN: But you are wrong if you think that it's all just about your mother. You might have noticed me doing all that once you got older. But you didn't notice it when you were a kid. Until you were fifteen and started closing your door at night, I used to come in to your room every night while you were sleeping, just to check you were still breathing. I used to hate going away for work because I just felt I needed you in the next room – wherever I was. Poor Mum never got to come with me on most of those trips because you had to be home for school and she was the only other person in the world I could trust to check your breathing. When she did come that once, I insisted we all go because I actually thought that if the plane went down, at least

	we would all die together. Thank God we weren't the Royal Family – they all have to travel on different flights.
ATHENA:	That explains it.
JOHN:	What, my anxiety?
ATHENA:	No. The Royal Family.
JOHN:	When Mum died, you said to me something about how close that connection is between parents and children. But it's not just the need for nurture. And it's not just about setting up insurance against being shoved into an old folks' home. It's about extreme companionship. We have all sorts of relationships in our lives. Friends, family, lovers, husbands and wives. We always think that the person we love, or make love to, is the most companionable. But I think when that person 'leaves' you come to understand something about your children that you really already know but never dare acknowledge.
ATHENA:	What's that?
JOHN:	That no one is closer to you, you love no one more and that you never ever want to be away from them. You know that warm feeling you get when you are buying socks in David Jones and you bump into your cousin who always used to laugh at you jokes? I get that feeling every time I see you. Every day, every time I come into your room to get my laptop back, every annoying time

you call me in the middle of a meeting. With everyone else, to some extent at least, you have to work on it. With you, it's the easiest thing in the world. It's really the only natural thing there is.

ATHENA: So you have to work on the unnatural bits of our relationship then.

JOHN: I suppose I do. *[Pause]* So when are you going?

ATHENA: How did you know they offered me the job?

JOHN: We would hardly be having this conversation if they hadn't.

ATHENA: Soon.

JOHN: You know, I can always put some money aside for your deposit if you settle for Lower Snug.

ATHENA: I know. Sometimes I think I'd prefer that.

JOHN: But then it's your responsibility to help me through this?

ATHENA: It is. The crushing responsibility of childhood. *[PAUSE]* Most often people really do come back you know.

End Act.

Entr' Act

[from The Merchant of Venice III.2]

JOHN [Sings]

Tell me where is Fancy bred –
Or in the heart, or in the head?
How begot, how nourished?
          Reply, reply.

It is engendered in the eyes,
With grazing fed, and Fancy dies
In the cradle where it lies.
          Reply, reply.

Let us all ring Fancy's knell.
I'll begin it – ding, dong, bell.
Ding, dong, bell.

End Entr'Act.

Act Five

It is early morning in an office at the embassy. MARGARET is sitting at a desk and has obvioulsy been there preparing for some time. Eventually JOHN enters.

MARGARET: Oh, you're here. Good morning, Mr Ferguson. Come in.

JOHN: Good morning.

MARGARET: How do you feel this morning?

JOHN: Fine, thank you.

MARGARET: Good. Please sit down.

JOHN: All right. Where are these papers? I don't want to spend any more time here than I have to.

MARGARET: Yes, I can understand that. It's hardly a sympathetic environment.

JOHN: Indeed. Now the papers?

MARGARET: Actually, there aren't any papers.

JOHN: What do you mean?

MARGARET: I don't have any papers for you to sign.

JOHN: Well, what the Hell did you get me down here for?

MARGARET: I thought it was important for us to go over things one more time.

JOHN: I have nothing more to say on the subject. I thought I made that patently clear the other day.

MARGARET: I don't think we managed to start off on the right foot the other day.

JOHN: Don't you? Well, I didn't give it another thought and, frankly, I resent you wasting my time like this.

MARGARET: I don't mean to waste your time.

JOHN: Well, you are wasting my time. Not to mention my energy. *[Giving a little more than he intended]* I don't think you really understand how incredibly draining this all is. I know I'm not frothing at the mouth or collapsing in a heap, but my body is in protest mode I can assure you.

MARGARET: I'm sorry.

JOHN: You don't have to be sorry. Just tell me there is nothing more needed of me and I'll be on my way.

MARGARET: There is nothing more we need and I really am sorry if you feel I've wasted your time.

JOHN: OK. Good. Thank you. *[He stands up]*

MARGARET: Thanks for coming to see us, to see me in the first place. You really didn't have to you know. And you are right. I can't imagine how you are feeling at the moment. It must be awful.

JOHN: I suppose, really, I'm still in a state of shock.

MARGARET: I suppose you are. In a sense the idea of that is really rather baffling. I'm sure the entire department and at least half the press at home are, sort of, counting on you feeling something like utmost clarity. But it doesn't sound like that is true at all.

JOHN: No. In fact, if this is shock, it seems that if ever I was in two minds they seem to have multiplied by about four. So many different scenarios now seem viable.

MARGARET: Whatever happened to 'when a man knows he is to be hanged in a fortnight, it concentrates his mind wonderfully'? But then I suppose you are not really facing the gallows or any other immediate fate.

JOHN: Not immediately no. *[He puts out his hand to shake hers. Just as she accepts he says...]* Tell me why did they send you?

MARGARET: What do you mean?

JOHN: Well, you are hardly head of department. What are you? Third secretary on your first posting? Let me see, eight years' nursing experience, followed by another ten child rearing, before you saw the ad in Saturday's

Age, paid your way into a Masters in International Relations, took advantage of some disadvantage or equal access policy and managed to make your way into the department from there?

MARGARET: That's completely wrong. It was teaching actually.

JOHN: Ah, teaching. Still nursing was a pretty good guess, given your current assignment. Anyway, was a third secretary with dubious credentials all I am really worth to DFAT?

MARGARET: Your daughter was a nurse, wasn't she?

JOHN: You know that.

MARGARET: Yes, I know that. In any case, you are probably lucky you got as high up the greasy pole as me. In fact, you're probably lucky you got anything more than a text message from us at all. You see DFAT doesn't have a position on this at all. We really don't. And we certainly don't go around getting involved in this kind of local matter just because there is an Australian citizen involved. *[He looks at her]* Two Australian citizens. Unfortunately, we can't do anything about your daughter and there is no other threat now to you or any other national, so that is about it for us. On balance the Minister would probably rather you did opt for clemency and take the money. He is a bit of a fascist, actually, but he can doubtless keep his more extreme right-wing constituents at bay by telling them you were persuaded by the not insignificant profit motive involved.

JOHN: That's pathetic.

MARGARET: Isn't it!

JOHN: I mean you, not the Minister.

MARGARET: What do you mean?

JOHN: Well, you're a parent. Any of your kids worth a million to you?

MARGARET: I wasn't suggesting that.

JOHN: No. You just thought it might be worth a final shot.

MARGARET: Oh, I don't know. I don't think I'm still working on this matter anymore. If I were I would have shut up a while ago, the other day even, and just finished the paperwork.

JOHN: So why are we still talking? Why did you get me here today?

MARGARET: I'm bound to say that I am just a little bit fascinated. It's a personal thing. As you say, I have children. I even have a daughter about the same age as yours. She's with me now, in fact, back at the hotel. I'm really intrigued to know what you are going to do. I once had dinner with the judge in the Ronald Ryan case and it was the same kind of fascination – except, apparently, he had less choice in the matter. You see no one can blame you for making either decision. You're kind of like a new millennium James Bond. You have a licence to kill, but you still come out of it look pretty good when you don't.

JOHN: But I'm not making a decision. I am doing nothing.

MARGARET: And the law, let alone the rest of society, has very little to say about people who do nothing.

JOHN: *Vertigo*? Something like that.

MARGARET: But I think you should make a decision. I really think you should.

JOHN: Why? What does it matter?

MARGARET: Because I think you will regret it if you don't. I think you have to. I think that if you are still around in 25 years you will actually think that the most horrific thing about all of this is the fact that you were the bloke forced to be in this position.

JOHN: What, more horrific than contemplating my daughter's murder?

MARGARET: Much more. Unfortunately, that happens to people every day. You are well read and a well-educated man. You know how people move on from things like this. They have to, otherwise they couldn't go on at all. And the prize they get is that, in the end, all they really remember is how pure their love is.

It may take decades, but I guarantee that, if you are still standing, it will be because you have been able to move on. *[Pause]* Your problem is that you have been cursed with the 'interesting dilemma'. If we were at home or even in some redneck backwater in the US, the matter would be totally out of your hands. We'd all be treating you like some sort of zombie and letting you see how this is really none of your business. What did Henry Bolte say with Ryan, "Victorians expect a hanging"? No, your problem is that in the middle of this crazy place you are being afforded the dignity of a decision. You have to make it. Otherwise you are dead.

JOHN: But I'm in shock as I told you. I can't make a decision in this state of mind.

MARGARET: What does shock feel like for you?

JOHN: I suppose I do feel like a bit of a zombie – except that my body is dead and my mind is working like mad. I can see every possible point of view at once.

MARGARET: That is perfect. Can't you see? Far better to be shocked, rather than passionate, when you are making this kind of choice. "Give me that man that is not passion's slave and I will wear him in my heart's core, ay, even in my heart of heart." Make your decision when every option is before you. Don't wait until you are blinded by revenge, remorse, guilt and especially not grief. What is more, make a decision. Life has given you this terrible burden and you have to take it on. You are doing it for all of us.

JOHN: I very much doubt that.

MARGARET: Sorry, but you know what you are? You're the moral scapegoat. You don't have a choice about that, I'm afraid.

JOHN: What do you think you'd do, if you were the moral scapegoat?

MARGARET: I hope I would do exactly the same as what you are going to do.

JOHN: But you don't know what I am going to do. You did before today, but even now you are entertaining the fantasy that your impertinent bit of rhetoric has moved me somewhat. That's got to be the beginnings of passion and that could lead to anything.

MARGARET: No. That was supposed to be the object of this morning's exercise, at least to get you to move so that you would take the clemency. But it hasn't turned out that way at all. I really have no idea. Not because I think I have moved you, but because I know now that unless I am ever in your exact position I will never have the moral capacity to make this kind of decision. That's why you can't just walk away without making a definite choice. The world needs to know and to see your clear intention. I suspect that someday you will need to be able to remember that too.

Act V

JOHN: Does anyone really care?

MARGARET: I do. In fact, I can't think of anything more worthy of care.

JOHN: So that's one.

MARGARET: Now you mustn't be full of yourself now that I have revealed your responsibility in this. Even I have a small part to play in this incredible burden. The decision has to be made by tomorrow and I am probably the last person who gets to speak to you about it.

JOHN: Do you want to put in a final bid?

MARGARET: No way. I have realised that I can't have any part of this – at least any further part. Once it's done, if I felt that I had contaminated your thought process in anyway it would have all been horrendously futile. But promise me one thing.

JOHN: What's that?

MARGARET: That when you make your decision you won't let yourself be distracted, in any way, from thinking about the way she died.

JOHN: Do you know the way she died? They told you all the details?

MARGARET: Yes. I never want to hear them spoken again, but I promise you, I will never, ever forget them.

JOHN: God help you.

MARGARET: *[Getting up to leave and offering her hand]* Goodbye. We'll probably never meet again.

JOHN: I suppose not.

MARGARET: It would be a bit of an anticlimax, I guess. *[Going to the door.]* I really am very sorry for you.

JOHN: I believe you are.

MARGARET exits. Lights fade somewhat and ATHENA takes up the position on the table she had in the prologue. JOHN walks downstage right to lean on the wall. He closes his eyes. Eventually ATHENA gets up from her slab, approaches him and puts her arms aroud him from behind. He does not open his eyes. Almost as soon as she has embraced him, she retreats, takes the sheet from the slab and walks offstage. Soon he looks back as if in hope of seeing her alive, but she has gone.

End Act.

Epilogue

Light fade up. JOHN is still in the same room, not quite able to leave. NINA enters.

NINA: Oh sorry, I was looking for someone.

JOHN: Not me?

NINA: No. Not you. My mother in fact.

JOHN: There's no mother here.

NINA: Right. I have obviously got the wrong room. She's meeting with a bloke, not you obviously. This bloke has to decide whether to take a million-dollar cash prize or watch some other bloke get his head chopped off.

JOHN: Yes, I heard that was in the building.

NINA: Yeah. Poor bloke is having a terrible time of it apparently.

JOHN: Why is that?

NINA: Well, the presumptively headless bloke raped and murdered our bloke's daughter.

JOHN: I see. Maybe that makes it simpler for him.

NINA: Maybe. But when you think about it, it is really not that much of a dilemma, is it?

JOHN: You don't think it matters?

NINA: Oh, I do. But only if he makes the wrong decision. *[Pause]* Anyway, you're not him or her, so I'd better keep looking. We're heading back to Canberra this afternoon.

JOHN: How delightful.

NINA: By the way, do you know Saudi very well?

JOHN: Only very little.

NINA: You don't know anything about tipping do you?

JOHN: Tipping?

NINA: Yeah. We have developed a bit of a situation in our hotel and as we are leaving in a few hours I want to know what to do. The bags are pretty full of duty free, you see, and I don't want to mess up my mother's diplomatic career by causing an international incident over tipping the luggage guy.

JOHN: I think in this country it's got to be worth at least 20 US.

NINA: Twenty? You think? I think I'd rather risk the incident. Anyway, see you in church!

NINA exits. JOHN sits at the table again thinking what to do. He resolves to accept clemency. In doing so his ambivalence rises up to the point where he slams his hand on the table in utter rage and self-loathing.

Lights fade.

Curtain.

www.ingramcontent.com/pod-product-compliance
Lightning Source LLC
Chambersburg PA
CBHW071320080526
44587CB00018B/3297